The Calming of the Storm

AMERICAN BIBLE SOCIETY
NEW YORK

The Calming of the Storm (Vol. 7)
Scripture quotes from the *Contemporary English Version,* Mark 4.35-41 (CEV).
Wording and grammar represent the kind of language best understood
and appreciated by young readers.

Copyright © 1995, American Bible Society
1865 Broadway, New York, N. Y. 10023
www.americanbible.org

Illustrations by Chantal Muller van den Berghe
Text by Bernard Hubler and Claude-Bernard Costecalde, Ph. D.
Design by Jacques Rey

Copyright © 1997, Éditions du Signe
Strasbourg, France

ISBN 1-58516-147-0
Printed in Italy
Eng. Port. CEV 560 P - 109864
ABS - 7/00 - 5,000

Jesus is not a magician.

So what is he, then?

His closest friends asked that question.

And Jesus used every opportunity to teach them and show them who he really is.

One day, while he was crossing the Sea of Galilee with them, there was a violent storm and they were afraid they were going to die. As you read these pages you will find out how Jesus set about showing his friends that he wasn't the same sort of man as the rest.

But who is this Jesus that everyone talks about and who attracts such great crowds?

Do you know him?

Jesus said to his disciples,
"Let's cross to the east side."

Jesus was worn out.
He had been talking to the crowd all day long.
He needed a bit of peace and quiet.
That's why it was better to go across
to the east side of Lake Tiberias,
also called the Sea of Galilee.

*If you need a bit of peace
and quiet, you have to get
away from the noise.*

They started across the lake with Jesus in the boat.

"Come on!" he said to his friends.
His friends were called disciples.
He got into the boat.
Some other boats followed him.
The sea felt calm.
No one said a word.
You could hardly hear the splashes
caused by the oars.

*You too have set out
on a great adventure.*

Suddenly, a windstorm struck the lake.

All of a sudden
there was a great gust of wind
and the sea was let loose.
The boat was tossed up and down
by the high waves.
The disciples began to panic.

*Everything seems calm and suddenly
a storm brews.
It can happen that way in your life too.*

Waves started splashing into the boat, and it was about to sink.

"Watch out, hang on!"
"Pass me that bucket. We need to get the water out!"
Everyone was rushing about.
The cries of distress coming from the disciples mingled with the great roaring of the sea.

What about you? Have you ever been really frightened?

Jesus was in the back of the boat with his head on a pillow, and he was asleep.

At the back of the boat
Jesus was sleeping peacefully,
his head resting on a cushion.
Of course, Jesus was really tired,
but how could he sleep
through all of this?

*Maybe sometimes you feel like
telling Jesus off for being asleep
when you are really frightened.*

His disciples woke him and said,
"Teacher, don't you care
that we're about to drown?"

There was panic on board
and the disciples couldn't understand
why Jesus went on sleeping
as if nothing was the matter.
They shook him really hard
to wake him up.
"The boat's sinking, we're going to drown,
and you're just sleeping?"

When you feel that you are in trouble
you can always call out to Jesus.

Jesus got up and ordered the wind and the waves to be quiet.

Jesus got up
and turned to face the sea.
He stretched out his hand and gave orders to the wind,
and he said to the sea, "Quiet! Be still!"

*Can your friends count on you
when they've got problems?*

The wind stopped and everything was calm.

At that very moment the wind fell.
The boat stopped rolling.
They managed to get the water out.
Everyone breathed a great sigh of relief.
They had been really afraid
that they were going to die.

You too know what it's like
when you calm down after a great fright.

Jesus asked them, "Why were you afraid?"

Jesus scolded the disciples for not trusting.
"Why be afraid if I'm here?"
They found it hard to understand
what had happened.

Lots of things happen around you.
Perhaps you don't understand them all,
but they can make you stop and think.

They were more afraid than ever and said to each other, "Who is this?"

The disciples still didn't know who Jesus was.
They would find out little by little.
They knew that only God can command the sea
and the wind.
So then? Could Jesus be the Son of God?
Isn't that what Jesus wanted them
to work out?

It takes time to get to know someone.
It takes time to find out who Jesus is.

What can we learn from this story?
Jesus always used ordinary events
to help his friends understand
what was important to him.
On the day of the storm he wanted to show his disciples
that he is the Son of God.
We too have storms in our lives:
when we have a fight with our friends;
when everything goes wrong at school;
when we get in a bad mood over nothing.
But Jesus will always be with us
to keep us from harm and to calm our fears.
We can trust him.

Jesus said to his disciples, "Let's cross to the east side."

They started across the lake with Jesus in the boat.

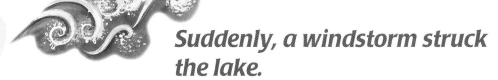

Suddenly, a windstorm struck the lake.

Waves started splashing into the boat, and it was about to sink.

Jesus was in the back of the boat with his head on a pillow, and he was asleep.

His disciples woke him and said, "Teacher, don't you care that we're about to drown?"

Jesus got up and ordered the wind and the waves to be quiet.

The wind stopped and everything was calm.

They were more afraid than ever and said to each other, "Who is this?"

Jesus asked them, "Why were you afraid?"

IN THE SAME COLLECTIONS:

The Good Samaritan
The Paralyzed Man
Zacchaeus
On the Road to Emmaus
Bartimaeus
The Call of the Disciples
Shared Bread
The Prodigal Son
An Amazing Catch
The Forgiven Sinner
The Farmer Who Went Out To Sow